Rails around Ireland
A Journey in Pictures
Compiled by Charles P Friel and Michael McMahon

© Images and Design: The Transport Treasury 2022 Text: Charles P Friel and Michael McMahon

ISBN 978-1-913893-16-3

First published in 2022 by Transport Treasury Publishing Ltd. 16 Highworth Close, High Wycombe, HP13 7PJ
Totem Publishing, an imprint of Transport Treasury Publishing.

www.ttpublishing.co.uk

Printed in Tarxien, Malta By Gutenberg Press Ltd.

'*Rails around Ireland*' is one of a series of books on specialist transport subjects published in strictly limited numbers and produced under the Totem Publishing imprint using material only available at The Transport Treasury.

Front Cover (1) – A busy scene at Dún Laoghaire's Carlisle Pier on Tuesday 5 July 1960 as J15 class 0-6-0 No.184 backs on to the 6.30pm Boat Train to Dublin Westland Row. The ship is the *MV Hibernia* which, along with sister *MV Cambria*, was built by Harland & Wolff in Belfast in 1948. She is seen here with the 5.45pm arrival from Holyhead. No.184 was built at Inchicore in 1880 and retained its saturated boiler and 1864-gallon tender until withdrawal in 1962. The locomotive was revived in 1967 for its part in the cinema film *Darling Lili*. No.184 is now owned by the Railway Preservation Society of Ireland (RPSI) who overhauled it in 1978 for its leading role in the cinema film *The First Great Train Robbery*. After 10 busy years on main-line excursions, No.184 is now a static exhibit at the RPSI's Whitehead Railway Museum in County Antrim. *FWG TT1664*

Frontispiece (2) – Belfast Great Victoria Street - Sparklingly clean GNR(I) PP class 4-4-0 No.75 is ready to depart from platform 3 of Belfast Great Victoria Street sometime between 1914 and 1919. Beyer Peacock of Manchester built fifteen PP class locomotives between 1896 and 1911 and the GNR(I) built two at Dundalk in 1911. The class was used at first on Belfast-Dublin passenger trains but was supplanted by the larger Q class after 1900. The PPs went on to be very successful performers on secondary lines. This locomotive was named *Jupiter* from new in 1898 but, like almost all GNR(I) locomotives, lost its name in 1914. No.75 passed to Córas Iompair Éireann in 1958 who promptly withdrew it. The bridge in the background had replaced Durham Street level crossing in 1863 and was itself replaced in 1936 (see picture 69). *Unknown TT1095*

Rear cover (83) – D14 class 4-4-0 No.88 lays a smokeseen as it runs round its train at Dalkey after bringing in a short suburban working from Dublin Amiens Street in 1956. Most suburban workings went to either Bray or Greystones but seven turned here daily. The siding on the down side, behind the signal cabin, was used for storing rolling stock, thus freeing up siding space at busier locations. A Park Royal coach can be seen at bottom left. Introduced by Oliver Bulleid in 1955, 50 kits of pre-fabricated parts were erected at Inchicore. The resulting 61-foot long carriage, with seats for up to 82 Second Class passengers, weighed just 26 tons and took full advantage of the more generous Irish loading gauge. For most of its length, the body was 10 foot 6 inches wide though this was reduced to 9 foot 6 inches at the ends. *Unknown TT1269*

Introduction

Selecting just 83 pictures from the archive of Transport Treasury for this book has been no easy task because what to leave out was even more challenging!

We present an approximately clockwise photographic railway journey around the island of Ireland, starting at Dún Laoghaire and finishing at Larne Harbour, using some pictures going back to the Great War, others from 1966, and everything in between. On the standard gauge, we visit the big concerns of Córas Iompair Éireann, the Great Northern and the Ulster Transport Authority as well as the much smaller County Down and the always-independent Sligo Leitrim. Ireland's narrow gauge lines appear courtesy of the Cavan & Leitrim, the "Wee Donegal", the Swilly, Tralee & Dingle and the West Clare but not in that order.

More than two-thirds of the photographs were taken in the 1950s, a period of great change on Ireland's railways. While modernisation and rationalisation were being planned, the rate of change was awfully slow to reach the more remote areas, particularly on the narrow gauge sections. Quite a few photographers from Great Britain made the pilgrimage to Ireland to record the "working museum atmosphere" that was disappearing back home.

We are thankful to all of the people who took the pictures and have credited as many photographers as possible. Unfortunately, almost all of their names have been lost over the years but the initials of fifteen different photographers did survive and appear here.

The tireless Henry Casserley led a group of eighteen Stephenson Locomotive Society members to Ireland and, although the party is named in the SLS Journal for June 1950, we do not know whether they are among the contributors here.

We have also used many pictures by the hard-working "Unknown" whose name appears here much too often. If you can provide any enlightenment, we will be happy to amend the records.

It is especially pleasing to be able to include pictures by outstanding local photographer William Robb who recorded much at a time when Ireland had only a few practising railway photographers. Many of his images in this book have not appeared in print since they were topical illustrations in a Railway Magazine of the time; one of his NCC pictures was, so far as we know, last published in October 1933!

We have tended to avoid the 'locomotive portrait' type of picture, preferring those images with a wider railway story to tell, be that signals, track layouts, carriages and wagons or the landscape. Having said that, some interesting pictures did not make the final cut because they just did not suit this format; either the negative was too lop-sided or badly exposed - or both! One attractive picture looked like the view from the cab of a Jeep banking a Mogul-hauled goods train near Mossley. But, on closer examination during the cleaning-up session, it turned out to be a Fairbairn tank banking a Black 5 on the Port Road of the Glasgow and the Sou' West. It is not here!

In our captions, we have tried to avoid telling the reader only what they can see for themselves and included some background, context and interpretation; hopefully enough to encourage you to find out more.

We hope that you enjoy the experience as much as we did putting it together.

Charles P Friel and Michael McMahon, September 2021

Abbreviations:

AEC - Associated Equipment Company manufactured mainly road vehicles but had partnered with Park Royal to build railcar bodies (based on Great Western Railway railcars) on AEC frames. The GNR(I) placed the first order for twenty railcars in 1950 and CIÉ ordered sixty similar cars in 1951. In 1946 AEC and Leyland Motors joined together to form British United Traction (BUT) who supplied a later series of railcars to the GNR(I).

CDR - The County Donegal Railway was an amalgamation of several railway companies operating 124½ route miles centered on Stranorlar and stretching to Strabane and Londonderry, to Letterkenny, Glenties, Killybegs and Ballyshannon. The English Midland Railway tried to buy the Donegal in 1903 which alarmed the Great Northern. The outcome was the CDRJC - The County Donegal Railways Joint Committee which was formed on 1 May 1906 and jointly owned by the GNR(I) and the Midland Railway. The Londonderry to Strabane section was transferred to the Midland Railway, later London Midland & Scottish Railway who continued to operate it through the LMSNCC until closure.

GNR(I) - The Great Northern Railway (Ireland) was formed in April 1876 through the amalgamation of many companies operating in mainly north-western and north-eastern counties of Ireland, and also linking Belfast and Dublin. It was perhaps the most progressive and enterprising of all the Irish railways.

GNRB - The Great Northern Railway (Ireland) retained its independent existence until the 1950s when the entire network was threatened with closure. The two Irish Governments stepped in with financial help and thus creating the Great Northern Railway Board on 1 September 1953 which lasted until 31 September 1958. The GNRB was disbanded following a savage round of closures, some of which were politically motivated by the road-minded Northern Ireland Government. The GNRB's assets were divided between Córas Iompair Éireann (CIE) in the Republic of Ireland and the Ulster Transport Authority (UTA) in Northern Ireland.

BNCR, MR(NCC), LMS(NCC) - The Belfast & Northern Counties Railway was taken over by the English Midland Railway in July 1903 who worked it through the Northern Counties Committee. The Midland Railway was amalgamated into the London Midland & Scottish (LMS) Railway in 1923 who continued to operate through the NCC. When the LMS became part of the Railway Executive in 1948 their operations in Northern Ireland were briefly part of the London Midland Region of British Railways. In 1949 the Northern Ireland Government purchased the NCC which became part of the Ulster Transport Authority (UTA).

UTA - The Ulster Transport Authority was formed in October 1948 with the merger of the Belfast & County Down Railway (BCDR) and the Northern Ireland Road Transport Board (NIRTB). The former NCC railway lines were added in 1949. The remaining open lines of the Great Northern Railway Board were taken over when it ceased to operate in October 1958; its assets were divided between the UTA and CIÉ. The UTA was always "anti-rail" and soon closed most of the former BCDR and NCC railway routes though some former GNR lines struggled on until 1965 when the road-minded lobby finally got their way. The UTA was in turn divided into road and rail divisions in 1968 when Northern Ireland Railways was created and the relentless purge of railways in Northern Ireland ceased and even reversed.

Dún Laoghaire Pier (3) – J15 class 0-6-0 No.122 waits on Thursday 14 August 1958 for passengers from the recently arrived *MV Princess Maud*. She was built by Denny Brothers of Dumbarton in 1934 for the LMS' Larne - Stranraer route and helped land the British Expeditionary Force in 1939. Believed to be the last ship to leave the Dunkirk Mole in 1940, she later landed American troops on Omaha Breach early on D Day in 1944. Based at Holyhead after the War to replace the Scotia, lost at Dunkirk, her lack of stabilisers and shallow draft made her unpopular with travellers. Locomotive No.122 was built at Inchicore in 1882 and had this "Z" type Belpaire superheated boiler fitted in 1942. She is here paired with a Type C tender which was first introduced in 1900 and was still being built in 1922. No.122 was withdrawn in 1963 and was scrapped at Dundalk. *FWG TT1683*

Dún Laoghaire (4) – C2 class 4-4-2T No.455 is at Dún Laoghaire at 7.45am on Saturday 3 May 1952 with a train for Dublin Amiens Street. The locomotive was the last one built by the Dublin and South Eastern Railway (DSER) at their Grand Canal Street workshops in 1911 as No.20 *King George*. Although intended for mainline trains between Dublin and Wexford, it was relegated to suburban duties as the 6'1" driving wheels were quite unsuited to the work. Two similar locomotives (DSER Nos.34 and 35) were supplied by Beyer Peacock in 1924 and they too worked suburban trains. Renumbered No.455 by Great Southern Railways in September 1926, the locomotive was withdrawn in 1959. At the time of the picture, there was only one through passenger platform at Dún Laoghaire until CIÉ built a platform on the up side in 1957, thus relieving an operational bottleneck. *MNB TT1345*

Dunleary (5) – CIÉ AEC railcar set, led by No.2653, was pictured on Tuesday 5 July 1960 heading south through Dunleary level crossing. This was north of Dún Laoghaire but south of Salthill, and close to the site of the 1834 southern terminus of Ireland's first public railway, the Dublin & Kingstown Railway. CIÉ used AEC railcars very similar to those of the GNR(I) but, instead of following their formation of one intermediate coach between a pair of powered railcars, CIÉ inserted two trailers. This placed extra strain on the engines and reliability suffered as a result. The second trailer here is a Park Royal; see outside back cover. Many of CIÉ's AEC railcars lasted until the mid-1980s but were much altered internally and had their engines removed for Dublin suburban work in push-pull mode with re-engined C class diesel-electric locomotives. The final few examples worked between Bray and Greystones. *FWG TT1666*

Dublin Westland Row (6) – At the south end of the station, ex GNR(I) U class 4-4-0 No.203 *Armagh* pauses during shunting operations in the bay platform on the down side on Saturday 2 July 1960. Meanwhile 257 or J4 class 0-6-0 No.258 departs Light Engine towards the Boston Yard which was on the Up side, just south of the station. No.203 was built by Beyer Peacock and passed to CIÉ in 1958. At this time it was based at the Broadstone from where it worked suburban trains between Dublin and Bray until withdrawal in November 1962. No.258 was one of a class of eight locomotives designed by R E L Maunsell and built at Inchicore in 1913-14. They were regarded as capable mixed traffic locomotives. No.258 was withdrawn in 1963 and scrapped at Dundalk. *FWG TT1663*

Dundalk 1 (7) – A relaxed scene at Dundalk locomotive running shed on Friday 24 September 1954 while crews chat around U class 4-4-0 No.202 *Louth*. The class had its origins in George Glover's five U class (Nos.196 to 200) delivered in 1915. With a light axle-loading, they could travel anywhere on the GNR(I) system, thus the white diamond on the edge of the front buffer beam. No.202, seen here, was one of the second batch of five which came from Beyer Peacock in January 1948. There were several differences including the square cab windows and being paired with E Type tenders. The new locomotives were delivered in the famous sky blue livery and were named after counties along the GNR(I) main line. The earlier locomotives were repainted to match and were named after loughs. No.202 passed to the UTA in 1958, was renumbered 67, and was withdrawn in May 1965. *EVF TT1136*

Dundalk 2 (8) – Pictured from the north end of Dundalk station's island platform on Friday 26 April 1957, 0-6-0 Crane Tank No.31 stands in No 31 Loop while shunting the carriage paint shops visible beyond the jib. A fairly typical Hawthorn Leslie crane locomotive, it was delivered in March 1928 for Dundalk Works. It always ran with an open wagon but the cab was cramped, so a coal bunker extension was added in April 1951. It seems to have worked for there are three people on the footplate here. When the GNR Board was dissolved in 1958, the Works was taken over by Dundalk Engineering Works Ltd. But they had little work for No.31 and it was sold to CIÉ in 1961. They renumbered it 365A in their departmental series and moved it to Inchicore. But its use there was short-lived, if at all, and it was scrapped in 1965. *Colin Bergstrand TT1369*

Diesels 1 (9) – Beginning with Railcar A in July 1932, the GNR(I) improved and innovated its railcars until F and G entered service in March 1938 and were used mainly on Howth locals. Two 102hp 6LW Gardner diesel engines each drove one axle of the central traction unit and could deliver speeds up to 48mph. Accommodation for 164 passengers and the guard was articulated fore and aft of the engine unit. This is a rear view, on Saturday 3 May 1952, of Railcar F departing Amiens Street for Howth, a fairly level 8¼ miles with five intermediate stops. Allocated to the Ulster Transport Authority (UTA) in 1958, Railcar F became their No.104 and was used mostly on Goraghwood - Newry - Warrenpoint services with a daily train to Portadown and back which included refuelling. It was withdrawn in 1965 when the Warrenpoint branch was closed. *MNB TT1450*

Diesels 2 (10) – The GNR(I)'s next step in railcar development was to order 20 single-ended power cars from AEC/Park Royal. Numbered 600 to 619, they were delivered between June 1950 and April 1951. They were designed to run in pairs with the even-numbered power car, with a Spanner boiler for train heating, at the Belfast end. The normal formation was two power cars with an intermediate coach converted from existing stock at Dundalk. These were mostly open saloon carriages though some were fitted to supply light refreshments. Here No.602 and No.603 shunt past the signal cabin at Dublin Amiens Street after working the 4.45pm express diesel from Belfast on Saturday 3 May 1952; the return of the 7.30am ex Dublin. The intermediate carriage here looks like K15 class Open Third No.93 of 1939 which would give the set a seating capacity of 24 Firsts and 134 Thirds. *MNB TT1433*

Diesels 3 (11) – CIÉ's B135 has just arrived at Dublin Amiens Street from Belfast Great Victoria Street on Thursday 31 August 1961. The 15 members of the B class (later B121 class) were built by General Motors in 1960 at La Grange, Illinois. They were their type GL8, single cab, diesel-electric locomotives of 950 horsepower with a Bo-Bo wheel arrangement, ie both axles in each bogie are powered. B135 entered service on 20 February 1961 and the class first worked cross-Border trains on 10 April 1961. B135 was just over 6 months old in this picture and is in its original grey and yellow livery. Note the oil lamp on the front bracket, the absence of handrails and air braking. The class almost invariably worked cab-first and had to be turned before the return journey. As 135, the locomotive was withdrawn in February 2003 and scrapped at Inchicore in April 2003. *SJH TT1036*

Diesels 4 (12) – The single-cab locomotives seen opposite were joined by a further 37 General Motors 950hp diesel-electrics in 1962. The newcomers were double-cabbed and thus independent of turntables. Here class leader B141 is being shunted at Dublin Amiens Street shed by ex-GNR(I) VS class 4-4-0 No.207 *Boyne*. This was on 11 June 1964, prior to No.207 working to Belfast Great Victoria Street with the Grand Steam Tour of Ireland. By then, A and B121 class diesels had meant that there was little work for No.207 and she had been sold in 1963 to the UTA when they were short of large locomotives. Although the nameplates had been removed, a fitter in Adelaide shed made wooden ones for *Boyne*. She survived long enough to work part of the Railway Preservation Society of Ireland's Inaugural Railtour on 11 September 1965 but was not preserved. Ironically, No.141 now does belong to the RPSI and is housed in Connolly shed. *Unknown TT1106*

Dublin Amiens Street 1 (13) – Designed by George Glover to replace ageing steam railmotors on suburban trains, this class of five 4-4-2T locomotives was delivered by Beyer Peacock in December 1913. Numbered 185 to 189 and known at first as Class T, they were the first of this wheel arrangement on the GNR(I) – and they had brakes on the leading bogie to help make sharper stops at suburban stations. After very successful superheating in 1926, twenty more (ten from Beyer Peacock and ten from Nasmyth Wilson) entered traffic between 1921 and 1930, classified as T2. Here No.185 is in the Howth Bay at Dublin Amiens Street (then platform 4 but now gone). The number painted high on the rear bunker suggests that the picture may date from before the Great War. No.185 was allocated to the UTA in 1958 and was withdrawn in a major cull of GNR(I) locomotives in March 1960. *Unknown TT1097*

Dublin Amiens Street 2 (14) – CIÉ No.402, a B2a class 4-6-0, starts away from the CIÉ side of Dublin Amiens Street station with the Belfast to Cork *Enterprise Express*. The service used two sets of carriages, one GNR(I) and one from CIÉ, which spent alternate nights in Belfast and in Cork. The GNR(I) carriages seen here had left Belfast at 10.30am and reached Dublin at 12.45pm. During the layover, the CIÉ locomotive shunted the set to platform 5 ready for a 1.45pm departure, arriving into Cork at 5.15pm after one seven-minute water and servicing stop at Limerick Junction. No.402 was the first of the 400 class to be rebuilt, in 1927, from four to two cylinders. It was 1938 before the GSR rebuilt the other six locomotives but not as comprehensively. No.402 was considered to be the best of the class but, ousted by diesels, was withdrawn in March 1961. *MNB TT1237*

Inchicore 1 (15) – Three combined locomotive and carriage units were built at Inchicore; No.90 in 1875 for the Castleisland Railway and two more in 1881. No.92 was the last one built and was the last to retain its carriage body. The other two were rebuilt as 0-6-0T locomotives; No.90 in 1915 and No.91 in 1924. No 92 is pictured at Inchicore signal cabin en route to Kingsbridge in 1938. Known as "The Cab", it provided a service for the more senior staff between Inchicore Works and Kingsbridge terminus. This quality turn continued until 1945. Sister No.90 is preserved in running order as a 0-6-0T at Downpatrick, Co. Down.
Unknown TT1295

Inchicore 2 (16) – Woolwich Mogul (aka K1 class 2-6-0) No.387 looks resplendent in the 1947 CIÉ green livery as it passes the castellated signal cabin at Inchicore with an up goods on Sunday 15 May 1950. The class was originally designed by Raheny-born REL Maunsell in 1918 when he was Chief Mechanical Engineer of the South East and Chatham Railway. After the Great War, Woolwich Arsenal had the unassembled makings of several locomotives on hand. The ever bargain-hunting Midland Great Western bought 12 kits of parts at £2,000 each which were erected at the Broadstone. The GSR bought a further 14 kits and other spares including boilers. These locomotives suffered from the same problems as their British counterparts and crews complained of rough riding, poor brake power, hot cabs and right hand drive. No.387 was withdrawn in October 1959, and was one of two Woolwich Moguls cut up at Dundalk. *HSB TT1336*

Inchicore 3 (17) – By the mid-1930s, heavier trains between Dublin and Cork were stretching the capabilities of the existing 4-6-0 fleet, particularly on the steep climb out of Cork. Earlier attempts by Inchicore to design a 4-6-0 were, at best, unsuccessful apart from the three members of the 500 class. Many suggested that an improved 500 would have suited better, but thinking at the time preferred 3-cylinder locomotives with larger driving wheels than the 500s. This is No.801 *Macha*, built at Inchicore in November 1939, the second of three 800 class locomotives which were the pride of Inchicore. Unfortunately "The Emergency", as the Second World War was known in Southern Ireland, intervened. Fuel supply problems (which lasted until 1948) meant that these fine locomotives were never really able to show what they were capable of. The advent of the diesels in the mid-1950s also meant less work on mainline services. *EVF TT1159*

Inchicore 4 (18) – The GNR(I) had considerable success with their AEC/Park Royal railcars, as seen in picture 10. CIÉ followed the GNR(I)'s lead and ordered sixty power cars from the same manufacturer. Nos.2600 and 2601 were the first to be built, in March 1952, and are pictured here at Inchicore in mid 1953. The last of the order was delivered in September 1954. The CIÉ railcars were very similar to their GNR(I) counterparts except that those meant for main-line use had tables fitted at the windows. Like on the Great Northern, much of the panelling covering the underfloor engines was replaced by wire grilles to reduce overheating and the risk of fire. No 2600 was converted for push-pull working in late 1973 and renumbered 6109. It was withdrawn in September 1981. No.2601 was re-seated in 1971 for Dublin suburban work but not converted for push-pull work and was withdrawn in 1975. *Unknown TT1030*

GS&WR Main Line 1 (19) – This is Thurles' down platform, looking towards Dublin, with the main station buildings on the up platform. D17 class 4-4-0 No.9 has just arrived with the Thurles portion of the 10.00am from Dublin Kingsbridge. The main part of the train reversed at Ballybrophy and then ran to Limerick via Nenagh. No.9's train had then served Lisduff and Templemore and, in turn, made a connection here into the following 10.30am Cork and Kerry which ran non-stop from Dublin to here. The operation was worked in reverse at 4.20pm when No.9 brought its small train back to Ballybrophy where it was attached to the same set of carriages from Limerick for a fast run to Kingsbridge. No.9 was designed by John Aspinall and built at Inchicore in 1886 as one of twenty members of class 52, built for express passenger work, principally between Dublin and Cork. *Unknown TT1032*

GS&WR Main Line 2 (20) – Originally designed by Watson as four-cylinder express passenger engines, B2 class 4-6-0 No.400 entered traffic in August 1916. It was the first of the ten in the class but they were not a success and three were withdrawn early, by Irish standards, in 1929 and 1930. The seven remaining locomotives were rebuilt with two cylinders between 1927 and 1938.as class B2a. No.404 and No.409 unofficially swopped identities in 1935 after orders had been issued to withdraw No.404. "The men" considered No.404 to be the better engine, so the numbers were switched and No.404 worked on as No.409 until March 1958. In this picture, No.404 as No.409 is departing Limerick Junction over the famous mid-platform scissor points with a train for Dublin Kingsbridge on Thursday 18 August 1955. *FWG TT1213*

GS&WR Main Line 3 (21) – The first two CIÉ mainline diesels were built at Inchicore in 1950-51. In 1956-57, they were joined by a class of twelve 960hp locomotives (B101-B112) built by the Birmingham Railway Carriage & Wagon Company. These had Sulzer power plants which CIÉ had intended for six twin-engined locomotives as part of their 1948 modernisation programme but which had remained in store because the Milne Report advocated constructing more steam locomotives! The wheel arrangement of "the Sulzers", as they were known, was A1A-A1A, ie the centre axle was not powered. B110 was introduced to service on 13 May 1957 and is here shunting at Limerick Junction on Monday 8 June 1964 opposite the mainline platform. It was stopped in November 1977 and, after a spell in the "sound barrier" at Inchicore, was cut up at Dublin North Wall in April 1988. *Unknown TT1114*

Limerick pilot 1 (22) – On Saturday 25 September 1954, CIÉ G3 class 2-4-0 No.291 (formerly Waterford Limerick & Western Railway No.44 *Nephin*) shunts a few wagons at the passenger platforms beside the Station Cabin. Designed by John G Robinson, of later Great Central fame, eight locomotives were built by Dübs in Glasgow and delivered between 1889 and 1894. Four were rebuilt by the GSR in 1925-26 and lasted until the 1950s. No.291 was withdrawn in August 1959 when it was the last Robinson engine in service in Ireland. *EVF TT1146*

Limerick pilot 2 (23) – D17 class 4-4-0 No.54 shunts carriages under the station roof at Limerick on Monday 8 August 1955. The engine may be confined to station yard work; there is a missing buffer head on the tender. Designed by Aspinall and built at Inchicore in 1883, this class was the first to be built with 6'7" driving wheels for express passenger work. Fans of the 1952 film *The Quiet Man* will recognise No.54 as a sister of No.59 which appeared in the film, particularly in the opening sequences. *FWG TT1177*

Cork Glanmire Road 1 (24) – CIÉ F6 class 2-4-2T No.36, designed by Ivatt and built at Inchicore in 1894, waits at Cork on Saturday 20 June 1953 with a suburban working for Cobh. At this time there were 12 trains each way between Cork and Cobh, an easy 12-mile run with six intermediate stops in a leisurely 30 minutes. No.36 was one of a class of six, two of which (Nos.35 and 36) had a step down in their side water tanks which reduced water capacity from 1250 to 1130 gallons. This was supposedly to improve sight lines for crews after a shunter had been injured. No.36 lasted until 1957 and was one of many locomotives sent to Spain for scrapping. *MNB TT1561*

Cork Glanmire Road 2 (25) – CIÉ General Motors locomotive B131 approaches from the Cobh Junction direction and is routed behind the passenger station. This is probably a "Run of Goods" bringing wagons to Rathpeacon where heavier trains were assembled, away from the worst of the climb out of Cork. B131 was one of seven of the class to enter service on 20 February 1961. The picture was taken after September 1966, when B131 and B132 were the first of the class to receive the new "Black & Tan" livery, but before the safety handrails along the "catwalks" were fitted. They were essential because checking the engine involved opening the louvered doors. The staff catcher on the cabside was used for Electric Train Staff exchanges on the former Midland Great Western lines between Dublin and Galway and Mullingar to Sligo. B131 ceased working in December 2001 and was cut up in March 2003. *Unknown TT1738*

Cork Expresses 1 (26) – We saw the Belfast to Cork *Enterprise Express* in picture 14. This is the return working waiting to leave Cork at 1.15pm on Saturday 20 June 1953, just before the service ended on June 27. Behind B2a class 4-6-0 No.401, the Great Northern carriages are led by L14 Third Brake No.192. This had begun life in 1943 as a K23 class workmen's coach seating 102 on slatted wooden seats but was rebuilt in 1946 to accommodate the Guard, 23' 1" of van space, and 30 Third Class passengers. Like the Down *Enterprise Express*, this train made only a seven-minute stop at Limerick Junction which allowed for connections from Limerick and, improbably, Wexford. Dublin was reached at 4.45pm, in time to form the 5.30pm to Belfast. The through train was replaced by a through coach from 29 June 1953 but that too was withdrawn on 19 September 1953. *MNB TT1233*

Cork Expresses 2 (27) – In a scene similar to the picture opposite but taken more than a year earlier, on Saturday 3 May 1952, the Dublin-bound *Enterprise Express* is again being worked by B2a class 4-6-0 No.401. Alongside is the 1.20pm to Tralee and Waterford which has an unidentified Woolwich Mogul piloted by D17 or 52 class 4-4-0 No.20 which dates from 1890. This train will follow the *Enterprise Express* and drop the pilot locomotive at Blarney before dividing at Mallow. The rear portion will reach Tralee at 4.40pm. The Woolwich Mogul will work the front portion over the hilly Scenic Route via Lismore and Dungarvan, to reach Waterford at 5.10pm. *MNB TT1231*

Rosslare Express 1 (28) – The up starting signal at Cork Glanmire Road is off for the 5.45pm (Saturdays only) Rosslare boat train on Saturday 20 June 1953. J15 class 0-6-0 No.182 double-heads Woolwich Mogul (aka K1a class 2-6-0) No.397 for the stiff climb out of Cork through the steep and damp 1355-yard tunnel and the long climb beyond through Rathpeacon. No.182 will be detached at Blarney and return Light Engine to Cork. No.397 will then be in sole charge, as seen opposite. Leaving Mallow at 6.27pm, the train was due alongside the boat at Rosslare Pier at 10.05pm. *MNB TT1443*

Rosslare Express 2 (29) – The Midland Great Western's purchase of twelve locomotive kits from Woolwich Arsenal in March 1923 has been mentioned earlier. The MGWR managed to erect only one set at the Broadstone before the formation of the GSR in 1925. The Great Southern erected the other 11 at the Broadstone before moving production to Inchicore where a further eight were assembled up to May 1929. Then, in late 1930, Inchicore produced another six locomotives but with 6 foot rather than 5' 6" diameter driving wheels. This brought the total of Woolwich Moguls in Ireland to 26. In this picture, larger-wheeled No.397 is taking water at Mallow while working the train seen opposite. No.397 was built in November 1930, fitted for oil burning in 1947-1948, withdrawn in November 1957 and sent to Aviles in Spain on 5 March 1958 for scrap as "a nominally working locomotive". *MNB TT1230*

Waterford 1 (30) – At Waterford shed in August 1954, D4 class 4-4-0 No.342 seems to be suspended in mid-air. The leading bogie has been removed and the front buffer beam is supported on a motley collection of wooden blocks. Meanwhile the back of the locomotive is hanging from the shear legs' crane - and the trailing driving wheels are gone too. *Al fresco* locomotive repairs like this happened at locations like Waterford and Cork Rocksavage depots especially when Inchicore Works was busy or when an engine was unable to work back to Dublin for attention. No.342 was one of five locomotives built at Inchicore in late 1936, an unremarkable 4-4-0 mixed traffic design, built without a clear purpose at a time of declining freight traffic and plenty of locomotives in service. All five were withdrawn in 1959 and No.342 was scrapped at Waterford. *Unknown TT1056*

Waterford 2 (31) – On Saturday 20 June 1953, No.334, another D4 class 4-4-0, is about to work the 7.35pm Mails and Perishable to Limerick, calling at all stations to Limerick Junction and arriving there at 11.20pm. The train waited at "The Junction" until 1.25am, shunting and allowing the 10pm and 11.15pm goods trains from Limerick to clear the 22-mile single line section before making a final intermediate stop at Dromkeen and arriving into Limerick at 1.40am. The Waterford crew worked as far as Limerick Junction and returned with the 10pm Mails and Perishables from Limerick. They arrived back in the Crystal City at 4.25am, a nine-hour rostered turn of duty. Here the crew is checking the sandboxes at what was Waterford's platform 7 at a time when there four bay platforms at this end of the station. *MNB TT1325*

Kerry branch 1 (32) – 101 or J15 class 0-6-0 No.195 (Inchicore 1898) waits at Glenbeigh with the morning mixed train in August 1954. This train had started from Tralee at 4.30am as a goods and waited at Killorglin from 7.41am until 9.07am to cross the 7.30am from Valentia to Tralee. During the Killorglin stop, the passenger coach was opened and the train then ran as a mixed as far as Cahirciveen. On this occasion, the passengers were accommodated in former Midland Great Western six-wheel tri-composite No.104M which had been built at the Broadstone in 1914. Glenbeigh was half way along the steeply-graded and very curved 39-mile branch from Farranfore to Valentia Harbour. The line was closed to passengers in February 1960, though cattle specials were worked until August 1960. *DTD TT1046*

Kerry branch 2 (33) – The train seen opposite arrived into Valentia Harbour at 1.35pm. After station work at the most westerly terminus in Europe, the locomotive worked back with the 2.25pm Mixed and Perishable train to Tralee. Here we see the new train, again with 104M next the engine, eight goods vans (aka covered wagons) and a goods brake van, as it battles up the five-mile climb – including many stretches of 1 in 50 and almost continuous curves – from Cahirciveen towards Kells and a further climb to the summit at the aptly named Mountain Stage station. The backdrop is Knocknadober (2267 feet). Its western side falls sheer into Dingle Bay, so the line had to run on this, eastern, side. *TT1050*

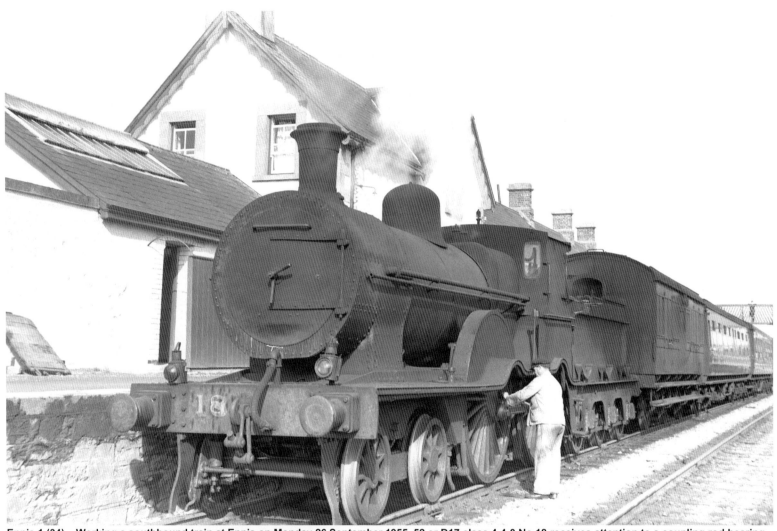

Ennis 1 (34) – Working a southbound train at Ennis on Monday 26 September 1955, 52 or D17 class 4-4-0 No.18 receives attention to a coupling rod bearing while working the 9am from Galway to Limerick. This train called everywhere except Longpavement which was "CR" (calls on request). Arrival at Limerick was 11.55am; nearly three hours' journey time for 73 miles! After leaving Galway, the locomotive would have run round its train at Athenry where potential Limerick passengers off the 7.45am from Tuam would have had nearly 90 minutes to make their connection at Athenry - enough time to view the town walls while having breakfast! No.18 was one of a class of 20 locomotives designed by Aspinall. It was built at Inchicore in 1888 and withdrawn in October 1959 before being cut up at Limerick in 1960. *AGE TT1263*

Ennis 2 (35) – Looking northwards along the narrow gauge West Clare Railway bay platform at Ennis on Wednesday 17 August 1955, the cramped West Clare yard can be seen curving to the left where Tourist saloon No.32 is beside the three-road carriage shed. The turntable was between it and the locomotive shed which has a Walker Brothers railcar of 1952 at home. The lean-to shed on its right was "The Breakdown Shed" which housed the diesel inspection car and emergency equipment. The West Clare's line to Moyasta Junction passed under the flat span road bridge while the standard gauge line towards Athenry went through the arched bridge on the right. The West Clare was threatened with closure in 1945 but was reprieved. Four Walker railcars came in 1952 and three F class diesel-mechanical locomotives in 1955. But it was not to last and the line closed on 31 January 1961. *FWG TT1209*

West Clare 1 (36) – Between 6 and 12 June 1953, about 40 members and friends of the Light Railway and Transport League ran a tour over many of Ireland's tramway and narrow gauge lines. On Wednesday 10 June 1953, the party visited the West Clare and used Walker railcar 3389 and railcar trailer No.48C to make the first (and probably only) non-stop trip from Ennis to Kilkee. Driver Michael Donoghue averaged 35mph and covered the 48 miles in 82 minutes 50 seconds. The ordinary stopping train was timetabled to take more than three hours – on a good day! This scene is at Kilkee after the railcar (with LRTL headboard on the radiator grille) had been turned, ready to work eastwards to the other terminus at Kilrush. It turned there too and then retraced its steps as far as Lahinch for a steam-hauled train back to Ennis – see opposite. *Unknown TT1073*

West Clare 2 (37) – Waiting at Lahinch was 0-6-2T No.5 with two Ennis-built vehicles; a 4-wheel passenger van and one of the West Clare's famous clerestory-roofed First Class saloons. No.5, formerly *Slieve Callan*, was one of three built by Dübs of Glasgow in 1892. She worked the West Clare's last steam-hauled passenger train in March 1952 and, in May 1956, appeared in the cinema film *A Minute's Wait*. Sent to Inchicore in July 1956, she lay neglected and was withdrawn in October 1959. But, in October 1961, a cosmetically-restored No.5 was put on a plinth at Ennis and a short section of the roof from Athlone Midland was added in the early 1990s. The locomotive was sent to Alan Keef at Ross-on-Wye for a full restoration and was steamed in July 2009 at her new home at Moyasta Junction where she is still active. *Hibberd TT1093*

Midland terminus 1 (38) – The Midland Great Western Railway introduced the distinctive K class 2-4-0 locomotives in 1893 for working their premier trains and the Limited Mails on the Mayo and Sligo lines. The twenty locomotives were later relegated to secondary lines and it is on such a duty that we see No.653 waiting to leave Loughrea on Saturday 31 August 1957 with a two-coach train on the 9-mile branch line working to Attymon Junction. When built at the Broadstone in 1894, No.19 *Spencer* had the distinctive "fly-away" cab which was not so enjoyable when travelling tender first! The fly-away cab was replaced in 1933 when the locomotive was re-boilered at Inchicore. The class was so successful that six were still at work in the early 1960s, among the last of the 2-4-0 wheel arrangement working anywhere in the world. *FWG TT1702*

Midland terminus 2 (39) – CIÉ ordered 94 diesel locomotives from Metropolitan Vickers in the 1950s. Sixty 1200hp Co-Co locomotives became the A class and the 34 C class were 550hp Bo-Bos. The A class arrived between July 1955 and January 1957. A58 had entered traffic in September 1956 and is here waiting at Westport on Wednesday 10 June 1964 with the 3pm goods to Athlone. Due there at 11.54pm, the train would take almost 8 hours to cover the 83 miles! A58 was rebuilt with a more reliable General Motors engine in May 1968 when it became A58R. It was stopped in April 1991 and scrapped at Inchicore in June 1995. The line alongside A58's train once extended a mile and a half to Westport Quay. The photographer on the right is standing on the stub of the 26¾-mile branch to Achill which closed completely in October 1937. *Unknown TT1116*

County Donegal 1 (40) – After 1906, the County Donegal Railway was managed by the Joint Committee (CDRJC) on behalf of the Midland Railway (of England) and the Great Northern Railway (Ireland). We start our visit at Donegal on Wednesday 11 August 1955 when a railcar, towing Trailer No 2 (from the Castlederg and Victoria Bridge Tramway) and a fitted van, has arrived from Strabane *en-route* to Killybegs. Soon, a railcar from Ballyshannon will arrive on the left and a Killybegs to Strabane railcar will come into the other platform. The tank wagon has diesel for the Ballyshannon railcar which turned five times each day on the turntable near the disused locomotive shed on the right. Three of the carriages beyond the tank wagon came from the NCC's Larne Boat Train of 1928 and may be waiting for specials to Rossnowlagh's Franciscan Friary on August 15, the Feast of the Assumption. *FWG TT1648*

County Donegal 2 (41) – Stranorlar as seen while looking east from the Ballybofey side of the River Finn on Saturday 19 May 1950. The Catholic Church of Mary the Immaculate is on the left and Stranorlar West signal cabin is to the right. Note that its back wall is fully glazed so that the signalman could see what was happening behind him. In the centre of the picture is ex-Dublin and Blessington Trailer No.3 sitting beyond the fine 210-foot girder bridge which carries the Glenties branch over the River Finn. The station here was on a long curve and the station entrance is marked by the triangular spire in the middle of the picture. The Glenties branch closed to regular services in December 1947 but was used by occasional goods trains until March 1952. The fine bridge, once destined for Norway, was cut up in 1955 when track lifting was completed. *HSB TT1463*

County Donegal 3 (42) – CDRJC Railcar No.18 waits below the spire of St Eunan's cathedral to leave Letterkenny for the 19¾-mile journey to Strabane on Thursday 10 August 1955. Letterkenny was the only place where the "Wee Donegal" and the Londonderry and Lough Swilly Railway met. The Swilly station was to the left of this picture and, though the systems were connected by a single spur to the east of here, there was little interchange traffic. Railcar No.18 was built in 1940 by Walker Brothers of Wigan and the body was built by the GNR(I) at Dundalk. It was rebuilt in 1949 after a fire. After closure, it was one of the vehicles purchased by Dr Cox for export to the USA but that move never happened and No.18 is now in service at Fintown on the former Glenties branch. On the right is evidence of Letterkenny's always-busy goods traffic. *FWG TT1646*

County Donegal 4 (43) – This was Raphoe on Saturday 25 April 1957 when Railcar 19 and a coach were arriving on a Letterkenny to Strabane train. After closure in 1959, Railcar No.19 and sister No.20 were purchased by the Isle of Man Railways where they survive though out of use. On the right is a 'Baltic', the nickname for all locomotives with a 4-6-4 wheel arrangement. This is CDR Class 4 No.14 *Erne* shunting goods wagons in the yard. After closure, No.14 worked the lifting trains from Strabane to Letterkenny where it was marooned. Purchased by Dr Cox (see picture 44), someone later painted it a dark, Swilly-like, green. It was kind gesture and it looked well but the vital "USA" letters disappeared. The scrapman was told to not cut up anything painted red and so the last Baltic in the British Isles was cut up in 1967. *Colin Bergstrand TT1547*

County Donegal 5 (44) – County Donegal Railway stock slumbers at the southern end of Strabane yard on Saturday 9 September 1962. That is the former GNR(I)'s Strabane South signal cabin on the left. Dr Ralph Cox from New Jersey wanted to re-create a section of the County Donegal Railway in New Jersey and, following closure of the CDR on 31 December 1959, he purchased four locomotives, three railcars, ten coaches, twenty wagons, thirty-four wagon chassis and one hundred tons of rails and fastenings to be brought across the Atlantic. Unfortunately the project failed. Nothing moved and the stock was left to deteriorate where it stood. CDR class 5 2-6-4T No 4 *Meenglas* (Nasmyth Wilson 1907), and a variety of carriages occupy the former CDR goods yard. *Meenglas* has been cosmetically restored and stands outside the Foyle Valley Railway Museum on part of the site of Foyle road station in Londonderry. *JLS TT1060*

County Donegal 6 (45) – In CDRJC days, the Midland's Northern Counties Committee had sole control of the 14-mile section between Londonderry Victoria Road and Strabane. Conveniently, the NCC also supplied all the coal needed, so railcars were seldom seen here. In this picture, one of the County Donegal Railway's five Class 5 2-6-4T locomotives (Nasmyth Wilson 1907-8) is leaving Victoria Road with a mixed train for Strabane. The class 5s were considered a very capable locomotives but there was some concern about their water capacity and the later class 5A locomotives had longer side tanks. The somersault signal, operated from the adjacent and exposed ground frame, is typical of NCC practice. The Craigavon Bridge of 1933 over the River Foyle is in the left background. Its lower deck enabled through working of wagons and vans between the Maiden City's four riverside railway termini, of two gauges.
Unknown TT1414

NCC 4-4-0s 1 (46) – In the 1890s, the Belfast & Northern Counties Railway followed fashion and began using compound 2-4-0s for its express passenger trains. No.50 *Jubilee* and No.55 *Parkmount*, built in 1895, were Worsdell-von Borries two cylinder compounds. They had seven-foot diameter driving wheels, the largest in Ireland, for express passenger work. But their tendency to vibrate at speed led to the leading axles being replaced with a bogie to make a more stable 4-4-0. No.50 *Jubilee* was altered to conventional simple working in 1926 but No.55 *Parkmount* remained in compound condition until it was withdrawn in September 1944 when it was the last surviving two-cylinder compound locomotive in the British Isles. Here we see *Parkmount* after arrival under the overall roof at Portrush. Note the tender weatherboard which was fitted in the 1930s for working the Magherafelt to Draperstown branch. Maybe this was an excursion from there? *Unknown TT1274*

NCC 4-4-0s 2 (47) – The shunting signal is off at Londonderry Waterside for U2 class 4-4-0 No.75 *Antrim Castle* to remove a bread wagon from the back of an arrival on Saturday 27 August 1955. The products of two Derry bakeries, Brewster's and Stevenson's, left the city overnight and the empty containers returned by late afternoon to do it all again. The U2s worked the NCC's principal express trains until the 2-6-0 Moguls began to arrive in 1933. No.75 was built in July 1924 by North British Locomotive Co and ran unnamed until in 1931. Only seven of the 18 U2s were built in Glasgow but locomen always called them "Scotch Engines". No.75 was last used in 1955 and scrapped in 1956 but sister locomotive No.74 *Dunluce Castle* – the first and last true "Scotch Engine" - survives, in LMS maroon livery, in the Irish Railway Gallery at Cultra, Co. Down. *BG TT1726*

UTA diesels 1 (48) – Multi Purpose Diesel (MPD) railcar No.36 is at the tail end of a departing service from Londonderry Waterside for Belfast York Road in April 1959, quite early in MPD times. The Ulster Transport Authority decided in 1956 to dieselise its passenger services between Belfast York Road and Londonderry with a journey time for the 92¼ miles in under two hours. Goods traffic was to be reduced and what remained was to be worked by the new MPD railcars which first entered service in September 1957. The normal MPD passenger train formation was up to four power cars, a dining or buffet car, and an intermediate coach. No.36 was a September 1957 conversion from UTA "Festival" coach No.321 seating 56 Third Class passengers which had been built as recently as 1951. No.36 struggled on until April 1978, replaced by new 80 class railcar sets built by British Rail in Derby. *Unknown TT1078*

UTA diesels 2 (49) – This is the Ganz railcar at Antrim on a working from Belfast York Road to Ballymena or Cullybackey. Designed by the Hungarian firm of the same name and built under licence by Metropolitan Cammell in Birmingham in 1937, it worked only a few test runs before going into storage. The UTA purchased it after the Second World War. Regauged, it made its first journey on 23 April 1951 between Belfast Queens Quay and Bangor. Officially No.5, but always known as "the Ganz", the car had a driving cab at each end and accommodation for 18 First Class and 36 Third Class passengers. An 80-seat trailer, No.215, was built in June 1953 to run with the Ganz but it was not a success. No.5 lay out of use in Adelaide shed for some time before being scrapped in Maysfields yard, Belfast in May 1965. *Unknown TT1079*

Swilly 1 (50) – Pennyburn locomotive shed in May 1953 with Londonderry & Lough Swilly Railway (LLSR) locomotives Nos.5, 3 and 2 nicely lined up. No.5 was one of a pair of 4-8-4Ts built by Hudswell Clarke in 1912, easily the largest narrow gauge tank locos in these islands. Nos.2 and 3 are part of a batch of four 4.6.0Ts built by Andrew Barclay of Kilmarnock in 1902. All three were funded by the Board of Works for the Londonderry & Burtonport Extension Railway. The Board of Works expected that the locomotives would be used on the Extension but the Swilly had other ideas, much to the frustration of the (remote) funders! The line west of Letterkenny closed in 1940 and the rest of the Swilly closed in 1953. Although little used towards the end, all three locomotives were offered for sale as working locomotives in 1954 but all went for scrap. *HSB TT1500*

Swilly 2 (51) – A tailboard rather than a lamp denotes the rear of a goods train leaving Pennyburn Station in Londonderry in May 1953, headed by 4-6-2T No.15 which was to work the final train just three months later. Just like the neighbouring CDR, a passenger brake coach was provided for the guard and anyone who wanted to travel. The Swilly's last regular passenger trains ran in 1948 but excursions, using the stock in the background of this picture, ran to Buncrana on Sundays and high days until 1951. These trains, which Derry folk called the *Budgen Express* (etymology unknown), sometimes ran to 13 packed carriages! The LLSR ceased running trains in August 1953 but continued to provide road freight services and a considerable network of bus routes. "Lough Swilly" buses could still be seen in Derry and Donegal up to April 2014 when the company went into receivership. *HSB TT1412*

Foyle Road 1 (52) – Delivered in February 1913, the five S class 4-4-0 locomotives from Beyer Peacock were certainly amongst Ireland's most handsome and popular locomotive classes. Designed to work heavier and faster expresses for the GNR(I) between Dublin and Belfast, they were very successful, and three similar S2 class locomotives were delivered in 1915. All eight were rebuilt at Dundalk between 1938 and 1939 - for accountancy purposes, they were "renewed". The original nameplates were restored to the five S class - and the three S2 locomotives received names for the first time. Londonderry Foyle Road is the setting for No.171 *Slieve Gullion* getting ready to depart with a train for Belfast Great Victoria Street on Friday 19 May 1950. No.171 is now preserved in running order by the Railway Preservation Society of Ireland at Whitehead, Co. Antrim. *HSB TT1247*

Foyle Road 2 (53) – Now looking south from the Craigavon Bridge mentioned earlier, we see a train leaving for Strabane and Portadown on Wednesday 10 August 1955. The Great Northern occupied a long, narrow strip of land here between the River Foyle on the left and Foyle Street on the right. The passenger station was behind the photographer and the locomotive shed is hidden beyond the goods store. To the left is one of the sidings which gave access to the lines of the Londonderry Port and Harbour Commissioners. One of the few surviving buildings today is the former Star Shirt Factory which is visible between the goods store and the goods office. The former factory is now a block of desirable apartments. The foreground here is now occupied by the Foyle Valley Railway Museum. *FWG TT1639*

GNR(I) 4-4-0s 1 (54) – At the south end of Strabane, under the footbridge connecting with the CDR, this is a Londonderry Foyle Road to Belfast Great Victoria Street train on Wednesday 10 August 1955. The carriage is GNR(I) No.40, the only K5 class Third with seats for 63. The locomotive is Qs class 4-4-0 No.125, one of a class of thirteen which were considered to be the Great Northern's first true express locomotives. Nine came from Neilson Reid and two from their successors North British Locomotive Co. between 1899 and 1903. The remaining pair were built by Beyer Peacock in 1904. All were named at first after either characters in Greek mythology or planets; No.125 had been *Daphne*. Rebuilding and superheating in 1920 made them even more popular with crews. Sister locomotive No.131 has been restored to main line operations by the Railway Preservation Society of Ireland. *FWG TT1635*

GNR(I) 4-4-0s 2 (55) – At Enniskillen on Friday 26 April 1957, just five months before total closure, PP class 4-4-0 No.44 rolls round the tight curve past the goods store to arrive at the up platform with a train from Omagh. The locomotive was built by Beyer Peacock in 1911 and was named *Leinster* before a purge of such frivolities after 1912. The first carriage is clearly narrower than the GNR(I) carriage behind. It was one of 19 ex London and North Western carriages purchased from the LMS between December 1947 and December 1949 and numbered 466 to 484. But only 17 of them entered service; No.466 and No.475 had such thin frames that they chafed the bogies and soon became lineside huts. Locomotive No.44 passed to CIÉ in 1958 and was withdrawn in February 1960. *Colin Bergstrand TT1278*

Sligo Leitrim 1 (56) – The Sligo, Leitrim and Northern Counties Railway (SLNCR) ordered two more 0-6-4Ts from Beyer Peacock, improved versions of locomotives already in service. Although completed in 1949, financial difficulties led to them being bought under hire purchase arrangements and they did not arrive until the summer of 1951. Beyer Peacock's ownership was declared on plates carried on the back of the coal bunkers, a little higher than the vacuum pipe. This is *Lough Melvin* approaching Manorhamilton with a substantial 2.15pm goods from Enniskillen to Sligo on Thursday 28 August 1957. The SLNCR closed at the end of September 1957 and both *Lough Melvin* and sister *Lough Erne* were purchased by the Ulster Transport Authority in 1959. The locomotives were given numbers for the first time, becoming 26 and 27 respectively. No.27 *Lough Erne* is on static display at the Railway Preservation Society of Ireland's Whitehead Railway Museum. *FWG TT1716*

Sligo Leitrim 2 (57) – In May 1950, eighteen members of the Stephenson Locomotive Society made a 760-mile, 9-day tour of railways in the northern part of Ireland. Here, on Thursday 18 May 1950, the guard looks from the front-entrance door in amazement at the line of photographers as SLNCR Railbus A leaves Manorhamilton for Sligo. This vehicle had been the GNR(I)'s D of 1934 and was sold to the SLNCR in June 1939 after the first Railbus A had come a poor second in a fight with a steam locomotive the previous March. The large luggage trailer was built at Manorhamilton in 1942 using the frame and wheels of a GSR Sentinel steam railcar. On the right is one of the line's many cattle wagons and clerestory-roofed bogie carriage No.10. It was the unlit member of the trio delivered from Hurst Nelson in 1924, funded by Civil War compensation money. *HSB TT1429*

Sligo Leitrim 3 (58) – The Sligo Leitrim left County Fermanagh in Northern Ireland at Belcoo and traversed four stationless miles through County Cavan in the Irish Republic before arriving at Glenfarne in County Leitrim. Here, Irish Customs officers inspected all traffic and examined – or rummaged – passenger luggage for dutiable items at the long tables on the platform. In this picture, on Thursday 28 August 1958, the Customs man is inspecting the contents of the trailer attached to 1938-vintage Railbus 2A while passengers wait until the process is completed. A typical rural scene complete with unlocked bicycles propped against the wall and a dog who probably knew – and was known by - everybody! *FWG TT1712*

Sligo Leitrim 4 (59) – On Thursday 18 May 1950, the Stephenson Locomotive Society group chartered Railcar B from Enniskillen to Sligo and back. It is seen waiting at Manorhamilton while the party visits the nearby SLNCR works. Built by Walker Brothers of Wigan and delivered to Enniskillen (via Omagh) in July 1947, Railcar B was great advance on the line's ancient railbuses with comfortable seating for 59 passengers, seated two-three style. Based at Enniskillen and almost invariably driven by Paddy Nevin, the articulated power unit was always at the Enniskillen end. The nearer sliding doors gave access to a spacious van space; no more trailers. The livery was an attractive regent green below the waist line, olive green above, and a white roof with the company initials at waist level. After closure in 1957, CIÉ purchased railcar B and renumbered it 2509. It is awaiting restoration at Downpatrick, Co. Down. *HSB TT1424*

Narrow gauge terminus 1 (60) – Timetabled passenger trains on the Tralee and Dingle ceased on 17 April 1939 though the famous monthly cattle specials continued until 27 June 1953. Just two weeks before that finale, on Thursday 11 June 1953, the Light Railway and Transport League visited as part of the tour mentioned earlier. Their special to Dingle and back was worked by No.8T (Hunslet Engineering, 1910) which was both the newest and most reliable locomotive. The special comprised bogie vehicles No.2T and No.5T which had been built by Bristol Carriage and Wagon in 1890 as Brake Thirds but converted to cattle use in 1940. Both had borrowed station seats for this occasion. After closure, No.2T went to the West Clare where it ran as 51C. No.5T became 22L on the Cavan and Leitrim before it too went to the West Clare. *Unknown TT1094*

Narrow gauge terminus 2 (61) – Cavan and Leitrim locomotive No.2L waits to leave Dromod with 4.30pm mixed train to Ballinamore on Friday 12 August 1955. Apart from conditional calls at halts, the only definite stop was five minutes at Mohill. One of eight 4-4-0Ts built by Robert Stephenson in 1887 for the opening of the line, No.2 was formerly named *Kathleen* after a Director's daughter. Preserved after the line closed in 1959, the locomotive is now in the Railway Gallery at Cultra, Co. Down. The first two vehicles of the train are ex Tralee and Dingle. First is van No.5T, the rear vehicle in the picture opposite, which came here in 1954 as No.22L. The second vehicle is T&D Brake Third No.18 (Midland Carriage and Wagon, 1907) which came here via the West Clare in 1954 as No.21L. It is now at the Pine Creek Railroad in New Jersey. *FWG TT1652*

Cavan and Leitrim visitors 1 (62) – Former Tralee & Dingle locomotive No.5T waits In the bay platform at Ballinamore on Saturday 13 August 1955 with the 1.50pm mixed train to Arigna. The train comprises two vans with carriage No.5L sandwiched between them. Built as a Composite, it had a guard's space inserted in 1945-46. Preserved by the-then Belfast Transport Museum, local members of the Irish Railway Record Society helped restore it to composite form. It is now at the Railway Galley, Cultra Co. Down. No.5T arrived on the C&L in November 1950 and was worked very hard until the line closed on 31st March 1959. It was subsequently preserved in the USA before returning to the Tralee & Blennerville Railway where it is currently stored out of use. In the distance, an ex-Cork, Blackrock & Passage locomotive is engaged in shunting while working the 12.20pm mixed from Dromod to Belturbet. *FWG TT1470*

Cavan and Leitrim visitors 2 (63) – Neilson & Co built four 2-4-2T locomotives for the Cork, Blackrock & Passage Railway in 1899 when that line was re-gauged from 5'3". Numbered 4 to 7, they were moved by the GSR to Inchicore in 1932 when the CB&PR closed. After some modifications, they were renumbered 10L to 13L and transferred to the Cavan & Leitrim section to supplement the line's original locomotives. Here at Ballyconnell in 1951, we see No.13L taking water while working the 12.20pm mixed train from Dromod to Belturbet, 2pm out of Ballinamore. The first two vehicles are Brake Composites No.6L and No.5L which had begun life as composites (see opposite). The locomotive was sent to Inchicore for overhaul in late 1951 but lay out of use there until it was scrapped in 1954. *RF TT1034*

Portadown local 1 (64) – GNR(I) T2 class 4-4-2T No.143 runs round its train at Armagh in April 1957, some six months before closure on 1st October. The timetable for that period has ten return workings between Armagh and Portadown though some started or finished in Belfast. No.143 was one of 20 T class locomotives; ten came from Beyer Peacock between 1921 and 1930 and Nasmyth Wilson built ten in 1924. No.143 was one of the latter and was withdrawn by CIÉ in 1963. The roof bracing spanning both tracks was similar to that at Newry Edward Street but the nameboard confirms that this is Armagh rather than Newry Edward Street – or yet another station at "Virol". *BHF TT1615*

Portadown local 2 (65) – GNR(I) PG class 0-6-0 No.151 (with a missing chimney cap) passes the goods yard, between Portadown Station and Portadown Junction signal cabin, with a two-coach train for Dungannon in August 1955. This locomotive was the first of the class of seven to be built. The GNR(I) built four themselves at Dundalk 1899 and 1904 while Neilson Reid built three in early 1901. No.151 began life as No.78 *Strabane*, was renumbered 151 in 1902 and superheated in 1921. Under UTA ownership it became No.151X before being scrapped in late 1961. On the right, GNR(I) AL class 0-6-0 No.29 has paused between shunts in the goods yard. This was another locomotive built at Dundalk, this time in early 1895. It carried the name *Enniskillen* until 1912, was superheated in 1918 and passed to CIÉ in 1958 but was withdrawn in October 1959. *BG TT1721*

Portadown 1 (66) – Pictured from the Belfast end of Platform One of Portadown's passenger station on Thursday 29 September 1962, two locomotives are at work in the carriage sidings on the down side. Nearer the camera is UG class 0-6-0 No.48 and further towards Lurgan is U class 4-4-0 No.68 *Down*. No.48 is stabling the two-carriage train used on locals to and from Dungannon while No.68 is preparing a lunchtime "advertised excursion" train to Bangor on the town's early closing day. Both locomotives were built by Beyer Peacock in 1948; No.48 was GNR(I) No.146 while No.68 began as GNR(I) No 205. Both locomotives carry the Ulster Transport Authority's livery of black lined red and straw. No.48 survived until June 1967 but No.68 was not so fortunate and was withdrawn in May 1965. *JLS TT1067*

Portadown 2 (67) – The final new steam locomotives on the NCC were the 18 Derby-built WT class 2-6-4Ts, derived from the Moguls in pictures 74 and 75. No.57, one of the final four in 1950, was on the Great Northern between May 1952 and June 1954 and again between 1960 and 1965. It is pictured here with the short-lived 2.30pm Belfast Great Victoria Street to Dublin between January and April 1965. That train was scheduled to be worked by a CIÉ Diesel Electric locomotive but, after the closure of the Warrenpoint branch and the Derry Road, plans often went awry. The location is Cumo accommodation crossing about a mile east of Portadown station. No.57 was stored in late 1965 and, after shunting at Belfast York Road in 1966, was again stored out of use. It was one of the first of the class to be withdrawn in March 1969. *Unknown TT1063*

Belfast 4-4-0s 1 (68) – GNR(I) PP class 4-4-0 No.71 is at Balmoral with a local train from Belfast to Lisburn. Clearly the fireman in new to the job for both safety valves are lifting; fingers crossed that there are no loco inspectors about! The locomotive was named *Bundoran* when new in April 1896 as one of the first three of the class to be constructed. Over the next 15 years, seven more batches brought the class total to 17, all but two from Beyer Peacock. The history of the PPs would be a study in itself but superheating made them excellent locomotives for working the many secondary lines including the former Irish North Western lines and on the Derry Road. The first carriage here is one of the former steam railmotors which dated from 1905 but converted to conventional use after 1913; all survived into the 1950s. *William Robb TT1004*

Belfast 4-4-0s 2 (69) – Five V class 4-4-0 three-cylinder compounds were introduced in 1932 for working heavier, accelerated express services on the GNR(I) Dublin – Belfast mainline. Named after birds of prey, they were given the famous blue livery after 1936 and Harland & Wolff-built Belpaire fireboxes after 1947. Here No.84 *Falcon* is waiting to leave Great Victoria Street on Sunday 14 May 1950. There being no *Enterprise* expresses that day, the rectangular nameboard on the smokebox handrail has been turned down. This is the 6.40pm train, due in Dublin at 9.50pm after calling at Portadown, Goraghwood, Dundalk and Drogheda. No.84 was allocated to CIÉ in 1958 and immediately withdrawn. But before being scrapped in 1961, it served as a stationary boiler for the former wagon shop at Dundalk Works where three-wheeled Heinkel Kabine cars were being produced. The bridge in the background (see picture 2) had been rebuilt in 1936. *HSB TT1584*

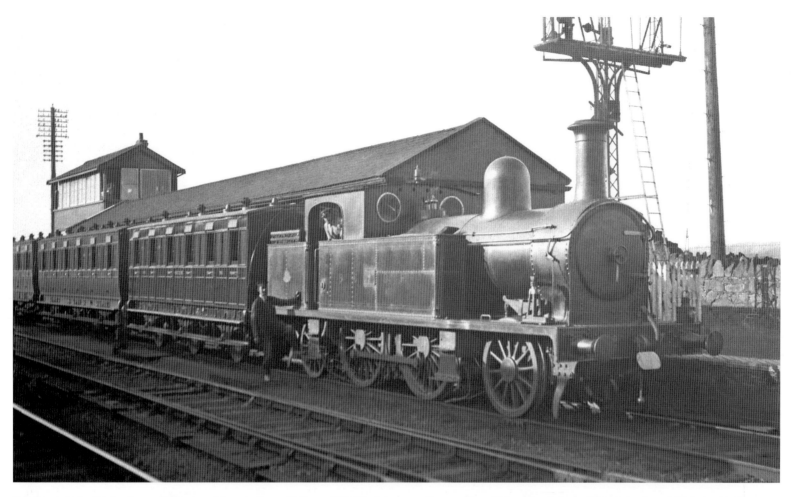

Comber 1 (70) – We begin our Belfast and County Down Railway (BCDR) pictures on the evening of Thursday 2 June 1932 at Comber. This is 2-4-2T No.7 (Beyer Peacock, 1896) which was given a new firebox in 1920 and became a regular on the Holywood Railmotors. These push-pull trains operated on the five level miles to Holywood but sometimes made the eight-mile trip to Comber which included five miles of climbing, some of it at 1 in 197. No.7, with a tailboard on the front drawhook, is ready to propel one such train back to Queens Quay. Something of a favourite, she was repainted in BCDR green by the UTA in February 1949 but severe damage to her bunker in a careless runaway that July led to withdrawal and she was scrapped in November 1949. The signal cabin on the left replaced Comber North and Comber South in 1925. *William Robb TT1008.*

Comber 2 (71) – Between 1928 and 1936, the BCDR brought huge crowds to the Ards Tourist Trophy motor car race; 410 miles in 30 laps around Dundonald, Newtownards and Comber. During the five-hour race, the BCDR also ran topped-and-tailed shuttle services between Comber and various viewpoints. Here, BCDR 2-4-0 No.6 has only one admirer at the Comber end of a shuttle train at No.3 level crossing, north of Comber, on Saturday 3 September 1933. That race, extended to 35 laps and 478 miles, was won by Italian ace Tazio Nuvolari but Omagh driver Hugh Hamilton came a close second after a botched pit stop. No.6 (Beyer Peacock, 1894) acquired a weatherboard in the 1920s for working the Ballynahinch branch which had no turntable. No.6 was returned to traffic in 1943 to meet war-time demands but the UTA closed most of the BCDR and No.6 last worked in January 1950. *William Robb TT1009*

BCDR suburban 1 (72) – Before the Great War, the BCDR's Locomotive Superintendent R G Miller asked Beyer Peacock to design a mixed traffic 2-6-4T. But, after two versions, the BCDR's Civil Engineer G P Culverwell wanted a symmetrical wheelbase - and got his way! Based on a design for Dutch State Railways, Beyer Peacock delivered four 4-6-4Ts, a wheel arrangement known as Baltic, in 1922. Their width confined them to the Bangor branch and Des Coakham described them as "beautiful coal-devouring engines that flattered to deceive". Firemen described them as miners' friends and often wished for a more economical, superheated, boiler. Here we see No.24 is stopped at Craigavad with twelve 6-wheeled coaches on a train to Bangor on Saturday 9 September 1933. After a stiff climb from Holywood, there is another half mile of 1 in 114 before the summit – and, unsurprisingly, the blower is hard on. *William Robb TT1010*

BCDR suburban 2 (73) – The BCDR also had busy suburban traffic on the main line to Comber and the Donaghadee branch. Here 0-6-0 No.26 pauses at Knock station in the Belfast suburbs with a lunchtime train towards Comber on Tuesday 4 July 1933. The trains is typically 6-wheeled carriages, something of a BCDR speciality, but with a bogie carriage towards the rear. Built by Beyer Peacock in 1892, No.26 was a "maid of all work" and, after a new boiler in 1920, could be found on all sorts of trains – from the fabled Golfers' Express to Newcastle to shunting coal wagons on Donaghadee pier or deputising for the diesel locomotive on the Ballynahinch branch. Queens Quay turned out No.26 in lined bright green livery in the 1940s but, after the UTA closed the main line on 15 January 1950, there was little to do and No.26 was scrapped soon afterwards. *William Robb TT1111*

Belfast York Road 1 (74) – More powerful locomotives were needed for the accelerated services over the NCC's new Loop Line between Bleach Green Junction and Monkstown which opened in January 1934. The solution was the W class of 2-6-0s, aka "The Moguls". Based on Fowler's 4P 2-6-4Ts for the LMS of 1927, the first four Moguls (No.90 to No.93) were built at Derby and delivered in July and August 1933. The remaining eleven Moguls were erected at York Road with parts from Derby and boilers from Crewe between June 1934 and October 1942. In this picture, No.95 *The Braid* of October 1934, with her wide chimney, arrives at York Road with a short train in 1939. The third vehicle is one of the two "halt coaches" which had begun life in 1904 as steam railmotors but were converted to tri-compo brakes in 1915 when their locomotives were declared "worn out". *JJC 1195*

Belfast York Road 2 (75) – Looking towards the buffers about 1950, W class 2-6-0 No.103 *Thomas Somerset* is waiting to leave platform three. No.103 was the penultimate Mogul, assembled at York Road in March 1942. The locomotive was named after the company Chairman who had established a large linen business and was also MP for North Belfast in Stormont. The background skyline was much altered in the Blitz attacks of 1941 when the station lost its overall roof and the Midland Hotel was all but destroyed. On the other hand, the platforms were extended to cope with wartime traffic. A huge scheme at York Road in 1926, saw Ireland's first use of colour-light signals with all points motorised and there was much use of flood lighting. A new signal cabin was opened on 5 September 1926 to control the revised layout and used 40 track circuits to monitor movements. *HSB TT1607*

Monkstown Junction 1 (76) – Work on the new Loop Line between Bleach Green Junction and Monkstown began on 1 January 1931 – though it had been advocated as long ago as 1872! The new line avoided reversals at Greenisland and trains to (and from) Portrush and Londonderry (Waterside) saved up to 25 minutes. In this September 1932 view, U2 class 4-4-0 No.84 *Lissanoure Castle* is propelling a train of materials south towards Bleach Green on the new up line. In the right distance is one of the concrete syphons which bring watercourses across the new cuttings. Behind the locomotive, the main line from Greenisland has been singled and diverted to a new alignment. Formerly, the main line was on the extreme left and at the same level as the photographer. He was standing on a new reinforced concrete bridge which had been cast in situ, in virgin ground, before being dug out. William Robb TT1002

Monkstown Junction 2 (77) – By May 1933, work was nearing completion when U2 class 4-4-0 No.75 *Antrim Castle* was photographed coming off what was to become "the back line" from Greenisland with, perhaps, Locomotive Inspector McDonald standing behind the driver. Note the temporary ground frame controlling the junction turnouts and trap points. The NCC built the line themselves, by direct labour, but borrowed narrow gauge tipper wagons from contractor George Cohen. At top left, sitting on the trackbed of the former main line, some of Cohen's wagons are awaiting return to their owners. No.75, like No.84 opposite, were two of the NCC's 18 U2 class locomotives. No.75 was built in Glasgow in 1924 and No.84 in York Road in 1929 using parts of A class No.20; it was named in September 1931. The Loop Line was opened on 17 January 1934 amidst much ceremony - and justifiable pride. *William Robb TT1020*

Larne Harbour 1 (78) – Unnamed U2 class No.73 sweeps in from Belfast in September 1939. Larne Harbour had both 5 foot 3 inch and 3 foot gauge tracks but, after narrow gauge passenger trains were cut back to Larne Town, the signalling here was revised and upper quadrant signals, rare items in Ireland, were installed in 1932. The signal cabin is to the right of the train. The mixed gauge tracks to the left allowed narrow gauge mineral trains from Retreat via Ballymena to reach the wharves via wagon turntables. Over to the right, alongside Harbour Road which was once Narrow Gauge Road, a narrow gauge train is ready to bring coal to the paper mill at Ballyclare. The large building to the right is the British Aluminium's Larne Aluminium works which had its own three foot gauge lines worked by three Peckett 0-4-0Ts (two of which survive!). *JJC 1202*

Larne Harbour 2 (79) – Beyer Peacock designed and built No.69 and No.70 for the Belfast and Northern Counties Railway in 1892. These two-cylinder compound 2-4-2Ts were renumbered 110 and 111 in 1897. York Road rebuilt No.110 in 1931 as Ireland's only 2-4-4T. The rebuild included a saturated version of the LMS G6 boiler and the only narrow gauge Belpaire firebox on the NCC. Although impressive looking, the rebuild was not a success. The firebox was much too small and No.110 was always short of steam. Her longer wheelbase caused frequent derailments and, under load, her weight fell back on the trailing bogie - and the locomotive slipped furiously. No.110 was confined to shunting Larne Harbour where she is seen in September 1939 with one of the 100 side-tipping ore wagons built in 1907 for the Parkmore iron-ore traffic. Hardly used during World War Two, she was withdrawn in February 1946. *JJC 1200*

Larne Harbour 3 (80) – NCC 4-4-0 class U2 No.73 simmers in the sunlight at Larne Harbour alongside the elegant brick and timber passenger terminal which, in 1890, was Berkeley Deane Wise's first design for NCC. The Stranraer boats are behind us and to our right. When the platforms were lengthened to cope with increased traffic in 1932, they had to cross the Shore Road. Two moveable platforms were devised which could be swung into place to link old and new and allow passengers to walk seamlessly to and from the steamers. The yard on the left gave both gauges access to the quayside. No.73 was built at Derby in 1922 as a U class 4-4-0 and rebuilt as a U2 at York Road in December 1937. It was to be named *Carn Castle* but the nameplates did not materialise. Withdrawal came in 1955 and it was scrapped in June 1956. *JJC TT1198*

Larne Harbour 4 (81) – We take our leave of Larne with this view of W class 2-6-0 No.96 *Silver Jubilee*, captured in classic rods-down pose, as it passes the outer platform while arriving with a nine-bogie train in September 1939. Heavy trains like this were common enough into Larne but, during the Second World War, a staggering 92,000 military vehicles and 4.3 million military personnel passed through here – as well as 754,000 civilians. The former narrow gauge platform had already been relaid to 5 foot 3 and a cattle dock provided a useful third platform. No.96 was named for the 25th anniversary of the accession of King George V and entered traffic in May 1935. It was the second of eleven Moguls to be built at York Road and the second to be withdrawn. It was last used in May 1955 but was not finally cut up until December 1961. *JJC TT1199*

NCC Flashback (82) – We close with this view of C1 class 2-4-0 No.51, in full NCC maroon livery, waiting to leave Coleraine with a train for Magherafelt, via Macfin Junction and the Derry Central line, sometime in the 1930s. The locomotive was built as C class two-cylinder compound No.21 by Beyer Peacock and delivered in December 1892. The class was the first use of Walschaerts valve gear on an inside-cylindered locomotive. No.21 was fitted for oil burning between November 1896 and 1901 and rebuilt with a five-foot boiler in 1928 and reclassified as C1. Confusingly, No.21 then swopped identities with sister No.51 of 1890 which had just been rebuilt as a B3 class 4-4-0. This was so that 2-4-0s and 4-4-0s could be numbered together. No.51, as it was after October 1928, was withdrawn in September 1938. *William Robb TT1012*